TREESOFHOPE

Saint: A Teen Boys Survival Guide On Body Safety Education

Copyright © 2021 by Trees of Hope

Published by Trees of Hope
    3901 West Broward Blvd., #122195,
    Fort Lauderdale, FL 33312

Email booksales@treesofhope.org for further information about Trees of Hope or for bulk orders.

All rights reserved. No part of this publication may be reproduced, stored in or introduced into a retrieval system, or transmitted, in any form, or by any means (electrical, mechanical, photocopying, recording, or otherwise) without the prior written permission of the publisher. Any person who does any unauthorized act in relation to this publication may be liable to criminal prosecution and civil claims for damages.

Cover and interior design: Nicole Escobar

First printing 2021

Printed in the United States of America

Print ISBN: 978-1-7367546-2-7

LIBRARY OF CONGRESS PUBLISHER'S CATALOGING-IN-PUBLICATION DATA

Names: Trees of Hope (Organization) | Escobar, Nicole, designer.

Title: *Saint: a teen boys survival guide on body safety education* / written by Trees of Hope; designed by Nicole Escobar.

Description: Fort Lauderdale, FL: Trees of Hope, [2021] |

Identifiers: ISBN: 978-1-7367546-2-7

Subjects: LCSH: Teenagers--Sexual behavior. | Sexual consent. | Sexual ethics for teenagers. | Teenage boys--Counseling of. | Dating violence--Prevention. | Online sexual predators-Identification. | Sexually abused teenagers--Services for. | Victims of dating violence--Services for.

Classification: LCC: HQ27.3 .S35 2021 | DDC: 306.7/08352--dc23

SAINT

A TEEN BOYS SURVIVAL GUIDE ON BODY SAFETY EDUCATION

WRITTEN BY TREES OF HOPE
DESIGNED BY NICOLE ESCOBAR

PUBLISHED BY

01.
PAGES 8-11
What Is Sexual Abuse?

02.
PAGES 12-13
Sexual Abuse Myths

03.
PAGES 14-17
What Is Consent?

04.
PAGES 18-21
Respect And Boundaries

05.
PAGES 22-27
What Is Puberty?

06.
PAGES 28-29
The Grooming Process

07.
PAGES 30-33
Drugs And Sexual Abuse

08.
PAGES 34-37
What Is Online Sexual Abuse?

09.
PAGES 38-41
What Is Teen Dating Violence?

10.
PAGES 42-43
The Problem With Pornography

11.
PAGES 44-45
What To Do If You Have Been Sexually Abused

12.
PAGES 46-47
How To Heal And Be Restored From Sexual Abuse

Knowing the facts about sexual abuse, how it applies to everyday life and what practical tools are helpful to strengthen vulnerabilities can have a significant impact on embracing the power of your safety.

Being a teen is an exciting stage of life when you have the freedom to embrace new experiences and shape who you want to be in the future. However, your teenage years are also the stage of life when you are most likely to experience sexual abuse. You have the power to be the exception by prevention strategies that prevent sexual abuse from darkening the freedom and independence that you deserve to grow as a person. Knowing the facts about sexual abuse, how it applies to everyday life and what practical tools are helpful to strengthen vulnerabilities can have a significant impact in enabling you to embrace the power of your safety.

PREVENTION MAGAZINE | SAINT 6

This prevention magazine has been created specifically to address the danger of sexual abuse faced by teenage boys in their everyday life and provide practical tools for establishing personal safety boundaries.

While reading this prevention magazine, we encourage you to think about situations in your everyday life that potentially make you vulnerable to being sexually abused. It's common to hear stories about sexual abuse and know the importance of the issue while also thinking that it would never happen to you. The real challenge is acknowledging that sexual abuse can be perpetrated anytime, anywhere, by anyone in your life.

Think about all the people you encounter in everyday life. This includes parents, relatives, classmates, childhood friends, family friends, neighbors, teachers, coaches, babysitters, youth leaders, and mentors. What type of relationship do you have with each person? Do you have someone who you feel comfortable enough to talk to about anything? Who provides the most support? Who has been the most helpful in previous times of need? Use these questions to start thinking about the trusted adults in your life who you can go to with any concerns.

What Is Sexual Abuse?

Sexual abuse takes place any time someone engages in sexual activity with another person that is not consensual. Most people believe that sexual abuse always involves rape, but the truth is that this type of abuse comes in many forms, including but not limited to rape, sexual assault, exposure, fondling, voyeurism, and commercial sexual exploitation. It includes touching and non-touching behaviors. Sometimes, sexual abuse doesn't occur between a teenager and an adult, but rather between teenagers.

Whether you attend private or public school, whether you're involved in sports or extracurriculars, whether you live in a "safe" neighborhood, whether you are in a romantic relationship - sexual abuse can occur anyplace, anytime, by anyone.

Contact Forms Of Sexual Abuse

- Unwanted touching, fondling, groping, cuddling.
- Sexual interactions while drunk or under the influence of drugs.
- Encouraging or forcing you to engage in a sexual activity.
- Coercing you to take your clothes off.
- Forcing you to touch someone else's genitals or masturbate. Feeling forced or pressured to have sex without protection.
- Forced or coerced penetration of a body part or putting an object inside the vagina, anus or mouth.
- Sexually touching you anywhere on the body, without consent, whether or not your is wearing clothes.

Non-Contact Forms Of Sexual Abuse

- Showing pictures, video or internet sites of pornography.
- Unwanted or unsolicited sexting.
- Leaking suggestive, nude, or explicit pictures and/or videos of you through text messages or social media.
- Forcing or coercing you to watch or listen to sexual activity.
- Voyeurism - inappropriately watching you dress or bathe.
- Sexually exploiting you for money, status or power.
- Sexually grooming and meeting you with the intent of abusing.
- Coercing you to pose for pictures or be in a video without clothes on.

How Common Is
Sexual Violence
Among Teens?

1 Statistics show that about 1 in 6 men experience sexual abuse before turning 18 years old.

2 Approximately 1 in 3 boys have reported feeling pressure to engage in sexual activities during their teenage years (Kaiser Family Foundation, 2003).

3 Research estimates that approximately 1 in 14 men have been coerced to penetrate someone else at some point in their lifetime (NISVS, 2015).

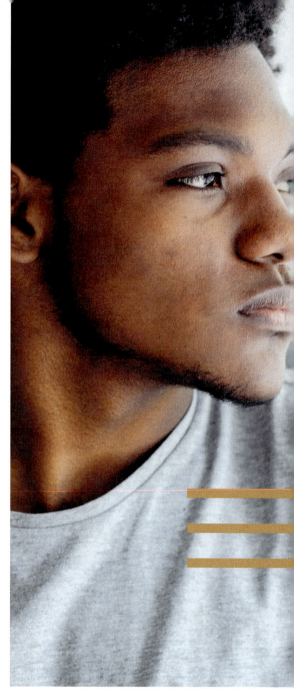

Symptoms Of
Sexual Abuse

Any sexual activity with a child or teen (by an adult or another child or teen) is sexual abuse. It causes physical and emotional pain, it has long-term effects and it is a crime. Recognizing childhood sexual abuse isn't easy. If you have been sexually abused, you may feel afraid and embarrassed to tell someone. If you have a combination of behavioral symptoms, physical symptoms, and reactions to different people and environments, you may have been sexually abused. We provide this list to help you have a better understanding of your experience and to get the help you need.

Behavioral Symptoms
Of Sexual Abuse

- Trouble focusing in school, extracurricular activities, or sports
- Nightmares and/or sleeping issues
- Anxiety and depression.
- Unhealthy eating habits along with significant weight loss or weight gain.
- Changes in personality and mood such as increased anger, fear, fatigue, or insecurity. This can also include different clothing style and changes in personal expression.
- Fear of being in certain places or around certain people for unknown reasons.
- Resistance to being alone with a specific person.
- Self-harming behavior such as increased drug use, binge drinking alcohol, cutting, and running away.
- Extreme worry regarding a girlfriend's expectations and reactions.
- Exhibiting adult-like sexual behaviors.
- Withdrawal from family and friends.

Physical Symptoms
Of Sexual Abuse

- Bruising or scrapes on the body.
- Pain, discoloration, bleeding, or discharge in the genitals, anus, or mouth.
- Soreness and/or difficulty walking or doing other physical activity. Sexually transmitted diseases.

Sexual Abuse Myths

Sexual abuse only happens with strangers.
- 93% of abuse is perpetrated by someone the victim knows. This can include people the victim loves and trusts such as family members, friends, babysitters, girlfriends/boyfriends, teachers, coaches, and youth leaders.

Sexual abuse is motivated by sexual desires.
- It is not only about sexual gratification; a perpetrator strategically targets their victim and takes advantage of their vulnerabilities to gain a sense of power and control.

Sexual abuse doesn't affect boys.
- Sexual abuse affects everyone. Remember, 1 in 6 boys experience sexual abuse by the age of 18. Boys can be sexually abused by other men and also women, regardless of sexual orientation.

If a boy experiences arousal during sexual abuse, it means he wanted it/enjoyed it.
- It's a normal physical response for the male body to experience an erection and ejaculation, even in a traumatic situation. The body's natural reaction does not mean that the abuse was wanted or enjoyed. Sexual abuse is never the victim's fault, no matter how the body reacts.

If someone says "yes" to sexual activity while drunk or under the influence of drugs, it counts as consent.
- State laws recognize that if a perpetrator uses alcohol or drugs to their advantage in order to impair the victim's control and prevent resistance, then sexual activity has happened without consent.

If a victim doesn't report the abuse right away, then it was not a big deal.
- Statistics indicate that 66% of teenagers who have been sexually abused did not disclose the abuse to their parents, other adults or law enforcement. Feelings of shame, guilt and fear can prevent victims from speaking up about abuse.

If a victim doesn't fight back, then it isn't considered sexual abuse.
- In traumatic situations such as experiencing sexual abuse, the victim can experience a fight, flight, or freeze response. Not fighting back is a natural response that the body and mind are using for protection.

You Can Be Vulnerable

Often, the majority of news about sexual abuse cases and rape trials are regarding female victims who were abused by someone they trusted. Exposure to this type of news makes it easy for a man to think "this would never happen to me" - until it does happen to you.

Since society expects that men are always the perpetrators of sexual abuse, it can be difficult for boys to disclose their experience as a victim of sexual abuse. The truth is that boys are vulnerable to the trauma of sexual abuse too.

Here some examples of situations which make teen boys more vulnerable to being sexually abused:
- Having your social media profiles open to the public.
- Spending alone/private time with older teens or adults.
- Lack of open lines of communication with parents.
- Neglecting to establish and enforce personal boundaries with adults and your significant other.
- Being under the influence of drugs or alcohol.

NO. 03

What Is **Consent?**

As a teen, you've probably heard "No means No" and that people should always ask for consent before sex. But what does consent actually mean and how can you apply it in your own life?

Consent is defined as actively agreeing and consciously saying yes to sexual activity or touching without pressure, manipulation, or being under the influence.

It's important to remember that consent is necessary not just for sexual activity, but also touching, holding hands, cuddling and kissing. Any sexual activity or touching that happens without consent is sexual abuse.

Although talking about consent may seem like it could "ruin the mood" or imply that you aren't experienced, it's important to remember that consent is empowering because it allows you to show that you respect your partner and that you understand body safety boundaries. A healthy relationship is built through open communication and the topic of consent should always be included in your conversations. Consent shouldn't be assumed just because you are in a relationship or based on the expectations of what "being manly" means, the kind of "vibes" you're giving someone, or what you have consented to in the past.

Think about how you know if someone wants to kiss you, or how you know if someone is ready for sex. Imagine if someone assumed you wanted to kiss them when you actually didn't. Your teenage years will involve receiving or giving confusing/mixed messages. The only 100% sure way to know is by asking, and having the person clearly communicate what they feel comfortable doing.

Every relationship is unique and every situation leading to intimacy happens differently. What if you really like someone and don't want them to feel rejected? What if flirting is fun but you aren't ready to take it to the next level? What if all of your friends have already had a sexual experience so you feel pressured to have one too? It's normal to have these types of questions and it's important to speak up and have these conversations with your partner about how you feel. Honesty and clarity about what you feel comfortable doing will help keep you safe and ultimately lead to having a healthy love life.

One "yes" doesn't apply to every type of sexual interaction. Consent has to be mutual and continuous - it's okay if you or your partner changes their decision. You have the right to choose which boundaries to set in place because your body is your own.

Consent becomes complicated when it develops into coercion. Coercion happens when you are being pressured, persuaded, intimidated, or manipulated into engaging in sexual activity or touching. For example, doing something you are uncomfortable with because you believe it's expected of you or because you believe you don't have a choice and can't safely leave the situation.

Remember that the lack of saying "no" does not automatically mean consenting with a "yes" and that no one should ever force you to turn your "no" into a "yes". The stereotype of being "manly" also places pressure on the man to make the first move, but it's essential to remember that you should never pressure anyone to engage in sexual interaction. As a teen who is going to be exposed to social situations such as parties or get-togethers, it's important to know that saying "yes" to sexual activity while under the influence of drugs and alcohol is not consent. Hookups often happen during parties or get-togethers as they provide a social space for flirting, "loosening up", and even an opportunity to drink some "liquid courage" to talk to that person you like. However, drugs and alcohol are inhibitors that impair judgment so consent cannot be legally given.

How To **Ask For Consent**

"How would you feel about this…?"

"Would it be okay with you if…?"

"Are you comfortable with this happening between us?"

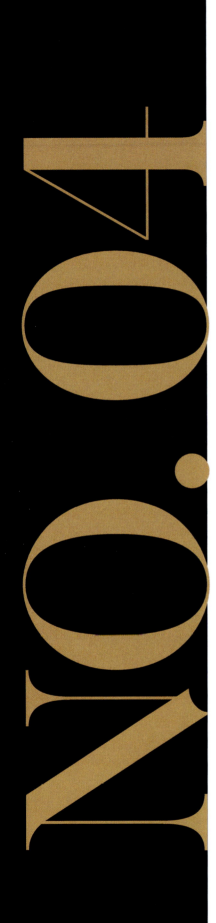

Respect & Personal Boundaries

Appropriate Touch

- High fives or fist bumps
- Side hugs from friends and relatives after asking for your consent (with their hand placed on your shoulder, not your waist).
- Holding hands with a significant other after asking for consent.
- Medical examinations:
  - Remember there should always be two people in the room.
  - If you are not comfortable with your parents being in the room during a medical examination, always ask for a nurse to be in the room so that you can eliminate the vulnerability of being completely alone with a doctor.

Inappropriate Touch

- Front-facing or tight hugs from adults such as relatives, teachers, coaches, and mentors.
- Placing hands around your waist, close to your butt, or close to your thigh or pelvis area.
- Perpetrators could use a hug to get closer to your body, and even pat their hands on your back or legs for sexual gratification.
- An adult or older teen encouraging or forcing you to sit on his/her lap.
- An adult or older teen going out of their way to give you a pat on the back, hug, tickle, or give a kiss on the cheek without doing it to anyone else.
- An adult or older teen giving you a massage or rubbing your back.
- "Fixing up" your clothes or athletic equipment while you are wearing them.
- Unwanted fondling, groping, stroking, or touching of your genitals and/or mouth.

Locker Room **Behavior**

School locker rooms provide an environment where it's just you and other boys, without any supervision or other authority figure. Most often, locker room behavior involves just playing around with friends and being foolish. Guys can be really loud, do some casual joking around, occasionally teasing and pranking each other. Locker rooms can be fun most of the time, giving you a chance to relax with your friends without teachers around.

However, some boys will try to show off their masculinity which can make the environment feel uncomfortable. Other boys will feel uncomfortable changing in front of others - it's important to understand that people need their privacy even in relaxed environments like a locker room.

With the #MeToo era, situations of any sexual or inappropriate touching are regarded as much more serious matters than ever before. It's important to remember the severity of disregarding personal boundaries and how it can affect your school and social life. It's helpful to understand that if something makes you uncomfortable, or you make someone else uncomfortable, it's always better to acknowledge and recognize the issue rather than blowing it off with a "boys will be boys" excuse.

How To Establish
Boundaries & Strengthen
Your Body Safety

PREVENTION MAGAZINE | SAINT 20

Here are some practical examples of how to protect your boundaries and avoid uncomfortable situations from becoming dangerous

- Avoid an unwanted hug by stepping backwards and saying that you're "not a hugger". This immediately creates physical distance between you and a potential perpetrator.
    - You can also prevent hugs by offering a small wave to signal hello/goodbye, or offering a handshake.
- Avoid being alone or in private with an adult or older teen. For example: if they offer special tutoring sessions or private practices, ask a trusted adult like a parent or close relative to accompany you.
- Embrace the courage in speaking up when someone's actions are inappropriate.
    - You can state "Your actions are making me feel uncomfortable and I would appreciate it if you would stop".
    - It's okay if the person gets defensive - you can further say that you are not focusing on their intentions, you are establishing your personal boundaries and that should be respected.
- It can be difficult to shut down someone's flirting attempts, especially when it's someone you know and you don't want to hurt their feelings.
    - Some ways to avoid uncomfortable situations. You can say that you just got out of a relationship and aren't looking for anything romantic at the moment. You can also say that you only want to focus on school and can't afford to have any distractions.
- If someone asks you to come over for some "Netflix and Chill", you can suggest using Netflix Party instead. It allows you to watch the same movie or show on Netflix while chatting on the side of the screen. This is a great way to have a movie date without putting your body safety at risk.
- It's a good idea to have a low key signal with your trusted friends so that they can save you from an uncomfortable or inappropriate conversation at a party.
    - If you don't have a specific "save me" signal, you can also text your friend to call you and make an excuse for needing you.

NO. 05

What Is Puberty?

Puberty is when you begin to experience physical, emotional, and hormonal changes as you develop into a more mature phase of life. Puberty happens to both boys and girls between 9 and 15 years old. Although puberty happens to everyone, it doesn't occur at the exact same time. It may feel weird, overwhelming, and confusing if you are the first of your friends or the last of your friends who is going through it.

Physical, Emotional And Hormonal Changes

During puberty, hormones will be released and signal the testicles to begin producing sperm and testosterone. Testosterone is the hormone responsible for the majority of the changes you experience.

These changes may make it feel like your world is normal one day and turned upside down the next. Your body will physically grow taller, growth spurts can last for a few years and end at your adult height. Other changes to expect include increased weight and muscles, your genitals will lengthen and widen, and your voice will experience spontaneous cracking until becoming deeper. Along with this, you will also begin to notice increased acne. Pimples mostly appear on the face and back, and most commonly range from blackheads to whiteheads to cystic acne. Although it may seem that they are never going to go away, your skin will improve with time.

Going through puberty also includes hair growth. Everywhere. Guys can start to grow more leg hair, arm hair, chest hair, armpit hair, pubic hair, and eventually facial hair such as beards, sideburns, and mustaches. You might also notice a new body odor that you haven't smelled before and feeling more sweaty. This is also due to hormones! In addition to physical changes, your emotions will become stronger and may feel overwhelming at points. Puberty can make your emotions feel much more intense than usual, and this can be hard to manage especially when you're put under so much pressure with school, friends, and your parent's expectations for your future. This can make even the smallest occurrences lead you to overthinking and reacting in ways such as having a short temper or constant irritability.

As a teen, you're faced with hard decisions every day, while your inner chemical balance is all over the place. A good tip when going through puberty is to not take yourself for granted. Look at what you love to do and all your talents - Are you good at sports? Are you good at singing or painting? How do you spend your time with friends? What activity helps you relax? Focus on everything you and your body can do can make going through puberty less overwhelming - it will become easier with time.

Puberty

Puberty is often seen as the process of becoming a man, but what does it mean to be masculine? Here are some stereotypes of masculinity:

- Having facial or body hair
- Speaking with a low voice
- Being fit and having muscles
- Hooking up with girls
- Being a "bro"

Sometimes it may feel like you are less of a man because your voice is high pitched, or you aren't making out with a lot of girls or having sex yet. It's important to remember that you're still developing as a man and

What Does It Mean To Be Masculine?

as a person. No one who is in their teen years has perfectly sculpted muscles or a full beard without any patchy areas - everyone is still figuring things out as they go. Full maturity is usually reached around the age of 25, so you still have a lot of time to figure out who you are, who you want to be, and how to get there.

Boys are also constantly pressured to identify being a man as being tough. Emotions are perceived as a girly characteristic, sensitivity is stereotypically seen as weakness. With hormones all over the place, there are bound to be guys who want to prove that they're not boys anymore, they're men. Proving this may seem like the biggest deal while you're in your teens but remember that there are a lot of other guys also going through hormonal changes - puberty is a phase of life that you will overcome. A powerful man is not defined through physical strength, aggressiveness, or dominance over others. Power comes from respect. If you embrace respect towards yourself and towards others, you will be able to become your most powerful self.

Masturbation

During puberty, you will begin to experience erections. This most commonly happens when thinking about or doing something that makes you aroused. It can also happen randomly without any reason due to hormones. The majority of teen boys begin masturbating around 12 years old. This is a new experience - it's normal for you to want to explore your body! You shouldn't feel ashamed or guilty for wanting to understand how it works and how it feels. During puberty, you might also experience wet dreams, which happen when you get an erection while you're sleeping and ejaculate. This is completely normal during the beginning stages of puberty as well. It's normal to want to learn how to deal with new sexual feelings through masturbation. Puberty is also the time when teen boys begin feeling attractions to teen girls by seeing them in a romantic or sexual perspective. As a teen, it's normal to develop crushes and to begin thinking about kissing and wanting to be in a relationship with someone you like. It's okay to ask someone you trust, such as your parent, about your curiosities.

Defining Values

There are hundreds of different ways to express and experience intimacy and love. Just because your friends are doing it one way does not mean you should feel pressured to do the same. Think about your role models. Whose relationships do you look up to? What do you look for in others? What do you want others to see in you?

You shouldn't feel pressured to meet the expectations of romance movies where the guy is portrayed as taking the initiative and being sexually dominant. However, asking if you can kiss or hold hands is not lame. On the contrary, it should be taken seriously because it's the most effective way to navigate dating and any sexual activity in a healthy manner. .

Sexual Curiosity

We know learning about sex can feel boring or embarrassing - it's easy not to pay attention or make fun of it. In addition, you have a world of information at your fingertips with internet resources to learn about sex and puberty, which may seem more relatable. But, in doing so, you may open yourself up to information that could be harmful. As awkward or overwhelming as it may seem, learning about sex, reproduction, and body safety from your parents or a trusted adult will be helpful to you in the future.

It's important to understand that it's normal to want to know about sex. As a teen, you might be asking yourself, "When is it okay to have sex?" First, think about your reasons for wanting to have sex.

Is it because all your friends have already lost their virginity? Is it because you feel like it's expected of you? Going through these questions can help you realize your motivation to have sex. You shouldn't need to have sex to feel cool or like you're grown-up. Having sex is a huge responsibility with many consequences that can be life-changing. Therefore, take the time to think about what you value and where you see your life going. Does having sex fit your values and life goals? Take all the time you need to learn about who you are and how you want to approach sex before acting on your desires.

NO 06.
THE GROOMING PROCESS EXPLAINED

One misconception of sexual abuse is that it happens spontaneously because a random stranger could not control their sexual desires. The reality is that the majority of sexual abuse is perpetrated through a long-term strategic manipulation of trust by someone the victim knows.

Identify And Target
Perpetrators can target a teen for grooming in school, in afterschool activities such as football, soccer, or swimming practices, in your neighborhood, and even in your own home. The grooming process will often start as a non-sexual friendship such as being a mentor, a friend you can go to when you don't want to talk to your parents, or a coach who is willing to provide extra practice to improve your skills as an athlete. Perpetrators will study your vulnerabilities such as your family life, friendship group, level of self-esteem, popularity and social media presence in order to gain access as a trusted person in your life.

Building Trust
Perpetrators know that the little things matter. Perpetrators will put in the effort to gain your trust through constantly admiring your skills, giving you advice about girls or sexual topics, and providing special attention only to you. This stage also includes giving special gifts that your parents might refuse to buy such as an Xbox, a Nintendo Switch, or AirPods. Perpetrators will also show interest by giving you access to things your parents may not, such as letting you drive their car and providing drugs and alcohol.

Isolation From Family And Friends
The more you depend on the perpetrator, the easier it is for them to maintain their abusive behavior for long periods of time. The perpetrator will attempt to spend alone time with you by encouraging you to disobey your parents, skip class, and miss curfew. Perpetrators will often offer you rides and special outings to disconnect you from family and friends. One warning sign that an adult may be grooming you for sexual abuse is when they make statements such as "No one understands you as I do".

Secrecy
The grooming process continues as the perpetrator encourages a sense of secrecy about your relationship with them. This will not only strengthen the bond they have to you but also decrease their chances of getting caught. Red flags to look out for in a conversation include the perpetrator saying "Let's keep this between us", "You are so cool for being low-key about us hanging out together", "We wouldn't want to ruin anything by telling others, right?"

Initiating Sexual Interactions
As a teen, you go through hormonal changes during puberty. Curiosity about your body and about sex is normal - but remember to be aware that perpetrators will exploit that curiosity, and use calculated strategies to manipulate you into sexual interactions.

Perpetrators can move on to sexualization by having you watch a movie with a sex scene in it, then progress to sending you explicit content showing sexual images or videos. They can even introduce you to porn as a way of "teaching you about sex". They will establish sexual touching such as a squeeze of your shoulder, offering a massage, helping you stretch your quads and hamstrings. Eventually, they will coerce you into a sexual interaction when you are in private.

Controlling The Relationship
In the final stage of the grooming process, the perpetrator will establish control over the relationship and your actions in order to continue abusing. For example, perpetrators can manipulate you into feeling shame or guilt about engaging in sexual activity. Perpetrators will also establish fear by saying "No one would believe you anyway" and threaten to share any sensitive information about you with your parents to get you in trouble.

Remember to trust your gut instincts. Although it is difficult to realize you are being groomed for sexual abuse during the process, keeping this information in mind when an adult or older teen is trying to establish a special relationship with you can be what makes the difference in keeping you safe from abuse.

The Link Between Drugs & Sexual Abuse

Perpetrators will use alcohol and drugs to lower their victims' inhibitions and take advantage of that vulnerability for sexual abuse. Substances commonly known as date rape or club drugs are a weapon of choice for perpetrators because they have no smell, color or taste - making it dangerously easy to slip into a victim's drink. Remember that date rape drugs can be used by anyone such as your close friends, family members, romantic interests, and trusted adults such as teachers, coaches, babysitters, and mentors.

Commonly Used Drugs & Symptoms

Alcohol

- Most common and easily accessible - mixing alcohol with other drugs in pill, liquid, or powder form can make the side effects even stronger.
- The pressure to drink at social gatherings can be used by perpetrators for abuse by taking advantage of your lowered inhibitions, impaired judgment, inability to provide consent and blurred memories.

Rohypnol (Roofies)

- Being roofied can cause symptoms of sleepiness, confusion, "blacking out" or "browning out" and decreased control over body movements. The effects of this substance can begin in as little as 30 minutes, peaking 2 hours after and lasting about 8 hours.
- Also known as circles, Mexican Valium, Forget-Me Pill, R-2, Roach, Roachies.

GHB (gamma hydroxybutyric acid)

- The effects of GHB attack the nervous system and can last up to 6 hours. GHB causes dizziness, throwing up, seizures, trouble breathing, heart rate problems, and even comas.
- Also known as Liquid Ecstasy, ILquid G, Georgia Home Boy, Cherry Meth, Goop, and Scoop.

Ketamine (Special K)
- Ketamine is a fast-acting drug often used as an anesthetic for animals. Dangerous side effects include hallucinations, reduced focus, and decreased sensitivity.
- Also known as Cat Valiu

MDMA (Ecstasy)
- Ecstasy is a stimulant that can provoke symptoms of hallucinations, decreased control over sexual restrictions, altered perceptions, teeth grinding and sweating.
- Also known as Molly, X, E, Essence, Hug Drug, Lovers Speed.

Combining alcohol and drugs impairs judgment and reaction time, and can severely decrease consciousness and memory retention even in small doses. Some signs that you may have suffered drug-facilitated sexual abuse include waking up with damaged or stained clothes, waking up without clothes, or physical symptoms related to sexual activity like soreness around the genital area and bruises or scrapes on arms or legs.

If you have experienced these symptoms and believe that you have been sexually abused, remember that it is not your fault. Someone has taken advantage of you and committed a crime against you. Statistics show that there is an increasing number of reports of drug-facilitated sexual abuse, so you are not alone. An important step you can take is to seek medical attention as soon as possible to determine what type of substance has been used and to help you recover from the side effects.

The best form of prevention is to avoid consuming alcohol and drugs.

However, if you do decide to drink, here are some tips to protect yourself:
- Make the drink yourself so that a perpetrator can't slip something in while making it for you.
- Don't chug straight from an already opened bottle.
- Never take your eyes off your drink - Don't give perpetrators the opportunity to place something in your drink.
- Hold the cup by the rim so that your palm covers the top of the cup. This decreases the chance that someone can place a drug in your drink without you noticing.
- Take your own alcohol and mixers to a party or drink from unopened cans of beer or alcoholic seltzers.
- You can use special drug-detecting kits that will change color when dipped into a spiked drink.
- Stay aware and use the buddy system so you and your friends can keep each other safe.

PEER PRESSURE PEER PRESSURE PEER PRESSURE PEER PRESSURE PEER PRESSURE PEER PRESSURE PEER PRESSURE PEER PRESSURE PEER PRESSURE PEER PRESSURE PEER PRESSURE PEER PRESSURE

How To Avoid **Peer Pressure**

As a teen, facing peer pressure is almost inevitable. Especially as a man, stereotypical ideals of aspiring to be as lit as frat boys in college who are always hooking up with girls can create increased peer pressure in social circumstances to drink and smoke weed.

Examples Of Peer Pressure Include:
- "If you don't take a shot, you're soft!"
- "We all smoke, it's no big deal just do it!"
- A group of people chanting for you to chug or drink.
- People trying to make you believe that you are less of a man if you haven't hooked up with a girl yet.

It's extremely hard to say "no" when you are in the moment. But remember, the truth is that not everybody is doing it. If you truly aren't comfortable, the bravest thing you can do is stay true to yourself and refrain from giving in to the pressure. It's also important to not be part of a group that pressures others. If you respect yourself, and if you respect others, they will learn to respect you and your decisions.

What Is Online Sexual Abuse?

Online sexual abuse is any type of non-consensual sexual activity that happens via the internet, text messages, social media applications, emails, online direct messages, and live streaming websites.

- Online sexual abuse can include coercion into sending and receiving sexual messages, images, or videos, grooming a target to meet in person for non-consensual or coerced sexual activity or touching, and being forced to watch or listen to sexual interactions online.

You wouldn't share personal or private information with a random stranger you just met on the street right? It's the same principle online. Even though it's satisfying to have a large number of followers and tons of matches on dating apps, it's best to protect yourself by keeping your online circle full of people you trust. It's safer to deny follow requests from strangers - the likes aren't worth the risk of being targeted for sexual abuse.

The National Domestic Violence Hotline reports that online abuse can lead victims to be twice as likely to experience physical abuse, and five times as likely to experience sexual coercion.

Keep in mind the type of relationship you have with someone in the real world as compared to the online world. Think about the type of behavior that is appropriate for teachers, coaches, mentors, babysitters, and other adults to have with you. Personal boundaries you have established with people in your life should also be respected online, and any inappropriate behavior should be immediately shut down and reported.

Dating Apps

The internet gives you the freedom to be whoever you want to be. Unfortunately, this gives perpetrators the opportunity to create a fake name, fake picture, fake profile and fake life in order to gain access to grooming you for sexual abuse.

Someone who is genuinely interested in you and in pursuing a romantic relationship with you will provide real information about themselves. Some ways you can tell if a profile is real is if they send you Snapchats of themselves or post stories of themselves with friends or family on Instagram or Facebook. If you notice them hiding their face or only posting pictures of food or generic places, that's a warning sign that they may not be who they claim to be.

You can do a reverse image search on Google to see if their picture belongs to someone else's social media account.

Also, with dating apps such as Tinder, there is an expectation that matching with someone and using the right pick up line will lead to casual sex. The majority of openers used are a variety of jokes about sex, oral, one night stands, boobs, etc. If you do use a dating app, starting with a raunchy pick-up line will most likely turn off whoever you messaged.

We encourage you to try to get to know someone organically, such as a classmate or a neighbor, and always maintain personal boundaries of respect. Although hooking up with as many girls as possible may seem like what is expected during your teens, building actual friendships first will help you in the future. If you do decide to use a dating app, remember that it's always better to use cheesy puns, introduce yourself, or say just a simple "Hey :)" if you really do want to meet someone. Be yourself.

Risks Of Live Streaming

Anyone can do a screen recording of a live stream. Even though you receive a notification if someone screenshots or records your content, once it has happened it's already too late. Avoid giving out personal information during a live stream as it can put you at risk of being targeted by perpetrators watching your broadcast. Don't allow anyone, even a significant other, to record or stream anything you want to remain private or are uncomfortable with.

The New York Times states that the reported number of images and videos of sexual abuse posted online was 45 million last year.

Sexting

Sexting includes sending partially nude or completely nude images through text messages or applications. It's important to be proud of your body; however, there are risks that come with exposing your private body parts online. Nude pictures can be leaked and end up on the internet for any perpetrator to see. Once someone takes a screenshot or saves that picture, there is no way to control whether it ends up online and who has access to your private images.

No one should ever pressure you into sexting. Sending nude pictures is not proof of how much you love someone or how good-looking you are. If you are ready to share that part of yourself with a significant other, make it special by doing it in person.

Pressuring you into sexting will often begin in subtle ways disguised as trying to get to know you better. For example, a perpetrator can ask you to play 20 questions and start by asking "What's your favorite color?" and "Are you a dog or cat person?", and eventually introducing sexual content such as "Are you a good kisser?" and "Have you ever had sex"? Perpetrators can also send you unsolicited nude pictures - if this happens, we encourage you to report the user to the application, to a parent or trusted adult, and to the authorities.

You deserve to have your privacy and boundaries respected online. Remember that it's not your fault if someone breaks your trust and abuses your right to a life free from sexual abuse.

Here are some solutions if any pictures or videos of you have been leaked online without your permission or consent:

1. Contact the website or application to have the content flagged as inappropriate and removed.
2. Talk to a trusted adult about the issue. You don't have to go into detail about the content, but they may have resources to help.
3. Remember that other teens have overcome online sexual abuse, and that there is hope for you to overcome it too.

Online Harassment

You should never feel forced to give your significant other access to your social media accounts or feel controlled in how you text, call or interact online with your friends. If your partner or romantic interest is constantly monitoring your online activity and texting you in a possessive way that interrupts your daily life and relationships with others, you can ask him/her for space. You can put your phone on do not disturb, block a contact who is harassing you, and deactivate all social media accounts where that person can reach you.

Helpful Online Tips To Tell Yourself

- Don't post your exact location on Instagram or Snapchat stories.
- Enable "Ghost Mode" on Snapchat so your location isn't available to others on its map feature.
- Make your Instagram, Twitter, and TikTok account private so only people that you approve can follow you and look at your content.
- Don't feel pressured to engage in any sexual activity just because it's expected from using dating apps. Take your time and really get to know someone before moving to the next level.
- Don't give out your personal phone number or home address publicly.
- If you've met someone online, check their mutual friends and their social media accounts before meeting them in person.
    - If something seems "off" or "sketchy", it's a warning sign that it may be risky to meet them in person before finding out more information.
- Everything is not what it seems. Trust your instincts, not the profile.
- It's always better to meet an online interest in public and have your parents or friends pick you up and drop you off.
- Report inappropriate content or fake profiles. Not only are you actively keeping yourself safe, but this also helps other teens from being targeted for sexual abuse.

NO. 9

What Is Teen Dating Violence?

Choosing to be in a relationship with a significant other means trusting that they will love and respect you. Unfortunately, that trust and sense of safety can be betrayed through dating violence.

1 in 3 teens has been a victim of dating violence and abuse in the United States.

Dating violence happens when an adolescent experiences physical, sexual, verbal, or emotional abuse from their partner. Here are some examples of how teen dating violence can happen:

- **Physical abuse:** Slapping, punching, kicking, using/throwing objects with the intent of hurting their partner.
- **Sexual abuse:** Forced and/or coerced touching, sexual activity, or digital intimacy.
- **Verbal abuse:** Screaming, belittling, name-calling, harassment through text messages, calls, and social media.
- **Emotional abuse:** Intimidation, threatening, bullying, humiliation, gaslighting, or isolation.

Sexual Abuse In A Relationship

Abusive girlfriends will use strategies of manipulation, pressure, and fear to gain power and control over their partner. Research from the National Institute of Justice in 2011 shows that 1 in 7 boys have been victimized by sexual coercion in their relationship.

Here are some ways that an abuser exploits their partners' vulnerabilities:

- Hacking into social media accounts and threatening to leak sensitive information.
- Pressuring and intimidating - such as pressure to have sex or do drugs.
    - Intimidation can occur through frequent arguing along with threats of breaking up if their partner doesn't give in to their demands.
    - Being in a relationship does not mean your partner can force you into sexual activities you do not want to do.
- Isolating their partner from friends and family.
    - Abusers want their partners to rely only on them. Abusers will take calculated steps to isolate their partner from anyone who threatens their control and power in the relationship.
- Lacking of respect for privacy or boundaries.
    - Abusers will take away their partners' independence by monitoring messages and social media, while also controlling their partners' social and personal life.

Approximately 1.5 million teenagers have been involved in risky, unsafe, and violent relationships. (CDC, 2006)

Tips On Building
Loving & Healthy
Relationships

Consent is key - always respect personal boundaries, remember that your body is your own.

Embrace your emotions and don't ignore gut feelings about how your partners' behavior affects you.

Remember that you are your own priority. If you notice warning signs of abusive behavior or experience violent reactions from your partner, put your safety first.

If you are in a unhealthy relationship, speak up and tell an adult that you trust - they can help you leave the relationship and start your healing journey.

Helpful **Reminders** To Tell Yourself

1. Someone who loves and respects you will never pressure you into doing something you're not comfortable with.
2. All relationships have problems; it's how you react to and overcome those problems that will shape your future with your partner.
3. Trust yourself.
4. Love involves building each other up, not tearing each other down.
5. Be brave in using your voice. Someone will listen.
6. You are not alone.
7. You matter.

Whether you are in the beginning stages of talking to someone or have been in a long term relationship for months or even years, you should never put pressure on them or be pressured by them to have sex or perform any type of sexual interaction. Remember, being someone's boyfriend doesn't mean you owe them a part of your body or control over your life - mutual respect is a key aspect towards building a safe and loving partnership between both people.

NO. 10

93% OF BOYS ARE EXPOSED TO INTERNET PORNOGRAPHY BEFORE THE AGE OF 18.

The Problem With **Pornography**

X-rated entertainment from sites such as Pornhub and OnlyFans don't portray realistic situations of sex, love, or relationships. Remember that the individuals you see in porn and people who create content on sites like OnlyFans, are making a profit from it. It's entertainment specifically created for specific types of viewers to fulfil sexual or relationship fantasies. What you may watch doesn't show behind the scenes - how a model or actor gets ready to make the video, their sexual relationships in real life, and how long the actual activity takes.

Pornography can also be used as a gateway to abuse, as a perpetrator can use explicit sexual images or videos to introduce sexual content into your relationship and exploit your curiosity to their advantage.

It's completely normal to be curious about porn and other x-rated entertainment. You may feel that it helps you learn how sexual encounters work, or helps you deal with girl anxiety. Just remember that those types of performances don't portray realistic situations of sexual activity, so it's better to prevent yourself from forming unrealistic expectations of sex.

Remember that your sexuality is still developing - so give yourself the best chance possible to develop a healthy sexuality that will help you in your future relationships.

NO. 11

What To Do If You've Been Sexually Abused

Reporting sexual abuse can be intimidating. Doubts about whether you might get into trouble, whether you'll be blamed and whether you'll even be believed can be overwhelming and discouraging. It's normal to feel confused, hurt, shocked, angry, or ashamed. The most important thing to remember is that it is not your fault.

Tell a trusted adult.
- Believe in yourself and speak up as many times as necessary until you receive the support you need.

Call 911 or report to law enforcement.
- Even if you were drinking, or if it was your partner, or if you feel responsible - a crime was committed against you and the main priority of law enforcement is ensuring your protection and future safety.

Seek medical attention.
- Hospitals often have trained medical staff who specialize in helping and treating people who have been sexually abused. Although immediately changing your clothes and showering might be the first thing you want to do, medical professionals recommend avoiding any type of cleaning or changing in order to gather important evidence.
- Although medical exams may feel embarrassing or intrusive especially after a traumatic experience, they will not be painful and can be instrumental for your physical healing.

Gather additional support from a counselor or a survivor-led healing group.
- Counseling professionals can help you through the healing journey and refer you to helpful resources.
- You are not alone. Many teens have experienced and overcome sexual abuse - there is hope for a safer future.

Understanding Your Feelings

Experiencing sexual abuse as a teen boy may make you feel disconnected from yourself, and flooded with emotions rooted in anxiety, guilt, self-blame, and shame. You may place the blame on yourself and question whether it was abuse or not if it was perpetrated by a female (such as a teacher or babysitter).

The stigma that men should feel happy or lucky to have sexual relations with a woman may make you feel doubt over how and why the situation happened, feeling like a "real man" would have not let the abuse happen, feeling like people will react differently to your story if the abuser was a woman. You're still young, and even if the abuser was a female and it feels like you entered the relationship with free will, the fact that they are older or hold some sort of power over you means that they had the ability to take your freedom to choose when and how you engage in sexual experiences.

You may also feel confusion over your sexual orientation because the abuse may have been stimulating and led to an ejaculation. How you reacted to the abuse does not make you guilty for it. Remember that it is never the victim's fault.

Your experience of sexual abuse and how it affected you does not define your physical strength, it does not define your sexual orientation, and it does not define your value as a man and as a person.

Remember that you are not alone. With time, you will be able to rebuild trust in yourself. You have the strength to overcome the abuse because you are deserving of a healthy and happy future.

NO.12

How To
Heal & Be Restored
From Sexual Abuse

PREVENTION MAGAZINE | SAINT 16

If you have experienced sexual abuse, **there is hope to breakthrough from being a survivor to being a thriver.**

Sexual abuse can provoke intense emotions and tormented thoughts such as blaming yourself, feeling shame that prevents you from speaking up and sharing your story, fearfulness of how others will see you if they know about your abuse, and feeling completely alone.

It's okay to acknowledge these feelings - they are not weaknesses, but rather a demonstration of your strength, courage, and will power towards beginning to heal. Remember that the only person to blame for sexual abuse is the perpetrator.

Remember that you are not alone. Your true friends and loved ones will listen to your story and counselors will offer guidance - many teens have survived sexual abuse, you can too.

Here at Trees of Hope, we want to help you overcome living life in the shadow of pain as a walking wounded and guide you through your healing journey towards a hopeful future. We encourage you to become involved in *Nobleman*, our customized healing program for teenage boys who have experienced sexual abuse.

Healing is your own journey. You have control over your body, your story, and your life.

Made in the USA
Middletown, DE
08 May 2022